T0055987

NOTE

THIS CELEBRATED composition by Giovanni Battista Pergolesi (1710–1736), one of the supreme masters of melody, was written in the last year of the composer's short life, and is commonly supposed (according to 'Grove') to have been commissioned by the confraternity of St Luigi di Palazzo at Naples, as a substitute for the setting of A. Scarlatti, which had hitherto been sung there annually on Good Friday.

It has been republished several times, but in the original it lies too high for any but mature voices. The present edition has therefore been designed to serve mainly for schools and Junior Festival Competitions. Care has been taken not only that the vocal compass should fit this purpose, but also that the transposed sequence of keys is such that the work can be performed satisfactorily as a whole.

The music is schemed by the composer for female voices (Canto I and II), strings, and continuo. No precise indication is given as to what was intended for solo or chorus treatment, but it is suggested that certain of the more florid movements should be sung by solo voices, both for practical considerations and to give variety in a complete performance; whereas other movements, such as the broader opening number, seem best fitted for chorus.

In the original the scoring for strings often follows the old custom of the second violin merely doubling the first violin, and the viola doing likewise with the bassi. The music has therefore been re-scored for strings so that each instrument may have an independent part. But as, in schools, viola players are seldom available, an attempt has been made in the present score to give fairly complete three-part harmony with first and second violins, and bassi; so that it can be played satisfactorily with only these instruments. If violas can be added, so much the better. This arrangement necessitates the original viola part being sometimes given to the second violins; but no substantial injustice is done, thereby, to the music. Score and parts, for use with this edition, are available, on hire, from the Oxford University Press, and the moderate difficulty of the string writing may well allow school orchestras to join in the performance of the work. With school choirs the Stabat Mater is already a great favourite.

With full string accompaniment a keyboard instrument may be dispensed with. If, however, it is necessary to 'fill in' or strengthen the sound, when the music is performed under chamber conditions with comparatively small forces, a harpsichord should be used rather than a pianoforte; but if a big choir and orchestra is concerned, then it is best to use the organ.

The keyboard part may be played as written in the vocal score though frequently it may be advisable to omit the melodic matter and play the harmony only. This, according to circumstances, must be left to the judgement of the conductor.

C. K. S.

(The chorus part is published separately)

STABAT MATER

1 Stabat Mater dolorosa,
Juxta crucem lacrimosa,
Dum pendebat Filius.

2 Cujus animam gementem,
Contristatam et dolentem,
Pertransivit gladius.

3 O quam tristis et afflicta,
Fuit illa benedicta
Mater Unigeniti!

4 Quae moerebat et dolebat,
Pia Mater, dum videbat
Nati poenas inclyti.

5 Quis est homo, qui non fleret,
Christi Matrem si videret
In tanto supplicio?

Quis non posset contristari,
Piam Matrem contemplari,
Dolentem cum Filio?

6 Pro peccatis Suae gentis,
Vidit Jesum in tormentis,
Et flagellis subditum.

7 Vidit suum dulcem Natum
Morientem desolatum,
Dum emisit spiritum.

8 Eja Mater, fons amoris,
Me sentire vim doloris,
Fac, ut tecum lugeam.

9 Fac ut ardeat cor meum
In amando Christum Deum,
Ut sibi complaceam.

1 Mother, bowed with grief appalling,
Must Thou watch, with tears slow falling,
On the cross Thy dying Son!

2 Through Thy heart, thus sorrow riven,
Must that cruel sword be driven,
As foretold—oh Holy One!

3 Oh, how mournful and oppressed
Was that Mother ever-blessed,
Mother of the Spotless One:

4 She, who grieving, was perceiving,
Contemplating, unabating,
All the anguish of her Son!

5 Is there any, tears withholding,
Christ's dear Mother thus beholding,
In woe—like no other woe!

Who that would not grief be feeling
For that Holy Mother kneeling—
What suffering was ever so?

6 For the sins of every nation
She beheld His tribulation,
Given to scourgers for a prey:

7 Saw her Jesus foully taken,
Languishing—by all forsaken,
When His spirit passed away.

8 Love's sweet fountain, Mother tender,
Haste this hard heart soft to render,
Make me sharer in Thy pain:

9 Fire me now with zeal so glowing,
Love so rich to Jesus flowing,
That I favour may obtain.

10 Sancta Mater, istud agas,
Crucifixi fige plagas
Cordi meo valide.

Tui Nati vulnerati,
Tam dignati pro me pati,
Poenas mecum, divide.

Fac me vere tecum flere,
Crucifixo condolere,
Donec ego vixero.

Juxta crucem tecum stare,
Te libenter sociare,
In planctu desidero.

Virgo virginum praeclara,
Mihi jam non sis amara;
Fac me tecum plangere.

11 Fac ut portem Christi mortem,
Passionis fac consortem,
Et plagas recolere.

Fac me plagis vulnerari
Cruce hac inebriari
Ob amorem Filii.

12 Inflammatus et accensus
Per te, Virgo, sim defensus
In die judicii.

Fac me cruce custodiri,
Morte Christi premuniri,
Confoveri gratia.

13 Quando corpus morietur,
Fac ut animae donetur
Paradisi gloria.

Amen

10 Holy Mother, I implore Thee,
Crucify this heart before Thee—
Guilty is it verily!

Hate, misprision, scorn, derision,
Thirst assailing, failing vision,
Railing, ailing, deal to me.

In Thy keeping, watching, weeping,
By the cross may I unsleeping
Live and sorrow for His sake:

Close to Jesus, with Thee kneeling,
All Thy dolours with Thee feeling,
Oh, grant this—the prayer I make.

Maid immaculate, excelling,
Peerless one, in heav'n high dwelling,
Make me truly mourn with Thee;

11 Make me sighing bear Him dying,
Ever newly vivifying
The anguish He bore for me:

With the same scars lacerated
By the cross enfired, elated,
Wrought by love to ecstasy:

12 Thus inspirèd and affected
Let me, Virgin, be protected
When sounds forth the call for me.

May the sacred cross defend me,
He who died there so befriend me,
That His pardon shall suffice!

13 When this earthly frame is riven,
Grant that to my soul be given
All the joys of Paradise.

Amen

Translated: BEATRICE E. BULMAN.

The purchase or hire of this work does not convey the right to perform, for which permission in the United Kingdom must be obtained from the Performing Right Society Limited.

PERGOLESI

STABAT MATER

No. 1 Chorus

Mother bowed with grief appalling

English translation by
BEATRICE E. BULMAN

Edited and arranged by
CHARLES KENNEDY SCOTT

* Original key F minor

Copyright 1927 Oxford University Press

Printed in Great Britain
OXFORD UNIVERSITY PRESS, MUSIC DEPARTMENT, GREAT CLARENDON STREET, OXFORD OX2 6DP

Photocopying this copyright material is ILLEGAL.

Orig.
mp
mp esp.
mf
- - - - - - - sa,
- - - - - - - ling,
Jux- ta cru- cem la- cri-mo- - sa,
Must thou watch with tears slow fall- ing
- - - - - - - sa,
- - - - - - - ling,
p
Dum pen-de- - bat
On the Cross thy
Jux- ta cru- cem la- - cri- mo- - sa,
Must thou watch with tears slow fall- - ing,
Dum pen-de- - bat
On the Cross thy
tr
pp
Fi- - li- us, Dum pen- de- - bat Fi- - li- us.
dy- - ing Son, On the Cross thy dy- - ing Son.
Fi- - li- us, Dum pen-de- bat Fi- - li- us.
dy- - ing Son, On the Cross thy dy- - ing Son.

*The grace marks in brackets may be omitted.

Orig.
f
p
f esp.
dum pen-de- - bat Fi- - li-us.
on the Cross thy dy- - ing Son!
Do- - lo- ro- sa.
Grief ap- pal- ling,
f
p
dum pen-de- - bat Fi- - li-us.
on the Cross thy dy- - ing Son!
p
f
p
mf
p
pp
p
poco
Dum pen- - de- - bat
On the Cross thy
esp.
la- - cri- mo- sa,
tears slow fall- ing,
Dum pen- - de- - - - bat
On the Cross thy
mf
p
pp
poco
p
Orig.
rall.
Fi- - li- us.
dy- - ing Son!
Fi- - li-us.
dy- - ingSon!
a tempo
rall.
poco rall.
p
mf
esp.
pp
mp
esp.
pp

CUJUS ANIMAM

No. 2 Soprano solo

Through thy heart, thus sorrow riven

* Original key C minor

Orig.
tr
mf
per tran- -si- vit gla- -di- us. Cu-jus a- ni- -mam ge- men-tem,
as fore- -told, Oh Ho- -ly One! Through thy heart thus sor- row riv- en
p
Contri- -sta-tam et do- -len-tem, Per tran- -si- -vit gla- -di- us,
Must that cru-el sword be driv-en, As fore- -told, Oh Ho- -ly One,
f
per tran- -si- -vit gla- -di- us.
as fore- -told, Oh Ho- -ly One!
sf
Cu- -jus a- -ni- mam ge- mentem, Con- -tri- -sta- -tam et do-
Through thy heart thus sor- row riv- en Must that cru- -el sword be
mp

-lentem, Per tran- - si- - vit, per tran- - si- -vit gla- -di-
driven, As fore- - told, as fore- - told,—Oh Ho- -ly
-us. Cu- jus a- ni- - mam ge- men-tem, Con-tri- - sta- tam et do- - len- tem,
One! Through thy heart thus sor-row riv- en, Must that cru- el sword be driv-en,
Per tran- - si- - vit, per tran- - si- -vit gla- -di- us,
As fore- - told, as fore- - told,—Oh Ho- -ly One,
rall. a tempo
per tran- - si- -vit gla- - di- us.
as fore- - told—Oh Ho- - ly One!
rall. a tempo
rall.

O QUAM TRISTIS

No. 3 Chorus

Oh, how mournful

*Original key G minor

con dolore
cresc.
O quam tris- tis et af- - flic- ta Fu- it
Oh, how mourn-ful and op- - press-ed Was that
O quam tris- tis et af- - flic- ta Fu- it
Oh, how mourn-ful and op- - press-ed Was that
leg.
il- la ben-e- dic- ta, ben-e- dic- ta Ma- - ter U- -ni- ge- - ni-ti!
Mo-ther ev- er bless-ed, ev- er bless-ed, Mo- - ther of that spot- - less One.
il- la ben-e- dic- ta, ben-e- dic- ta Ma- - ter U- -ni- ge- - ni-ti!
Mo-ther ev- er bless- ed, ev- er bless-ed, Mo- - ther of that spot- - less One.
poco rall.
a tempo
Ma- - ter U- ni-ge- - ni- ti!
Mo- - ther of that spot- less One.
Ma- - ter U- ni-ge- - ni- ti!
Mo- - ther of that spot- - less One.
a tempo
poco rall.
cresc.

QUAE MOEREBAT

No. 4 Soprano solo

She who grieving

*Original key E♭ major

et do- - - le- bat, Pi- a Ma-ter, dum vi- de-bat
was per- - - ceiv-ing, Con-tem- - pla-ting, un- - a- bat-ing,
Na- - ti poe- nas, poe- nas in- cly-ti, Pi- a Ma-ter,
All the an- guish of her Son, Con-tem- - pla-ting,
Orig.
dum vi- - de-bat Na- - ti poe- nas, na- ti poe- - nas
un- a- - bat-ing, All the an- guish, all the an- - guish
in- - cly- ti, Pi- a Ma-ter dum vi- - - de-bat
of her Son, Con-tem- - pla-ting, un- a- - - bat-ing,

p cresc.
f
Na- - ti poe- nas, na- - ti poe- - - nas in- - cly- ti.
All the an- guish, all the an- - guish of her Son!
p
f
sf
p
(tr) (tr) (tr) (tr)
mf
Quae moe- re- - bat et do- -
She, who griev- ing, was per- -
mf
p
mf
p
-le- bat, et do- - -le- bat,
-ceiv- ing, was per- - -ceiv- ing,
Pi- - a Ma- ter,
Con- tem- plat- ing,
p
mf
p
dum vi- - de- bat, dum vi- de- bat,
un- a- - bat- ing, un- - a- bat- ing,
p
Pi- a
Con- tem- -
mf
p

mf
p
cresc.
f
Ma-ter, dum vi- - de-bat Na- ti poe- nas, na- ti poe- - nas
-pla-ting un- a- - bat-ing All the an- guish, all the an- - guish
mf
p cresc.
f
p
mf
in- - cly-ti, Pi- a Ma- ter, dum vi- - de-bat
of her Son. Con-tem- - pla-ting, un- a- - bat-ing,
mf
p
mf
p
cresc.
f
rall.
Na- ti poe- nas, na- ti poe- - nas in- - - cly- ti.
All the an- guish, all the an- - guish of her Son.
p cresc.
f
rall.
f
esp.e rit.
mf
mf
dim.
p

QUIS EST HOMO

No. 5 Duet

Is there any

*Original key C minor

molto esp e rit.
Quis est ho-mo,
Is there a- ny
- len- - - - - - tem cum Fi- li- o ? Quis non pos-set
suf- - - - - - f'ring was ev- er so? Who that would not
rit.
qui non fleret, Chris- - ti Ma- trem si vi- - der- et In
tears with-holding, Christ's dear Mo- ther thus be- - hold- ing In
con- - tris-ta-ri Pi- - am Ma- trem con-tem- - pla- ri
grief be feel-ing For that Ho- ly Mo-ther kneel- ing,
tan- to sup- pli- ci-o ?
woe like no other woe?
rall.
Quis, quis?
Who? who?
Do- - len- tem cum Fi-li-o ?
What suf- f'ring was ev-er so?
Quis, quis?
Who ? who?
rall.
dim.

PRO PECCATIS

No. 6 Chorus

For the sins of every nation

*Original key E♭ major

pp
f
-tum. Vi - - dit Je - - sum in tor-
prey: She be - - held His trib - u -
-men - tis, Et fla - gel - lis sub - - -di - tum, Et fla-
-la - tion, Giv'n to scour - gers for a prey, Giv'n to
cresc.
mf
-gel - lis sub - - di - tum.
scour - gers for a prey.
pochiss. rall. a tempo
p
rall.

VIDIT SUUM

No. 7 Soprano solo

Saw her Jesus foully taken

Original key F minor

(tr)
più p
-en- tem de- so- la- tum, mo- ri- - en- tem de- so- la-tum, Dum
-ing, by all for- sa- ken, lan- guish- ing, by all for- sa-ken, When
più p
dim.
pp
e- - mi- - sit spi- - - - ri-tum.
His spi- rit passed a-way.
mf
dim.
pp
dim.
mp
esp.
Vi- - dit su-um dul-cem Na- tum
Saw her Je-sus foul-ly tak- en
p
mp
mf
f
p
Mo- - ri- en-tem de- so- - la- - tum, de- so- la- - - tum, Dum e-
Lan- guish-ing, by all for- - sa- - ken, all for- sa- - - ken, When His
mf
f
p

mf
sf
-mi - - sit spi - - rit - um. Vi - - - dit su - - um dul - - - cem
spi - - rit passed a - way. Saw her Je - sus foul - - - ly
Na - tum Mo - ri - en - tem de - so - la - - tum, de - so - la - - - tum,
ta - - ken, Lan - guish - ing, by all for - sa - - ken, all for - sa - - - ken,
p
pp
dim.
Dum e - - mi - sit, dum e - - mi - sit spi - - ri -
When His spi - rit, when His spi - rit passed a -
- tum.
- way.
mp
esp.
ppp

EJA MATER

No. 8 Contralto solo

Love's sweet fountain

*Original key C minor
(*)The grace notes in this number should be rendered as in the pianoforte accompaniment

meno f
render
p
f
p esp.
vim do- lo- - ris, Fac, ut te- - cum lu- - ge-
soft to ren- - der, Make me shar- er in thy
meno f
p
f
p
f
p
f
-am, lu- - ge- am.
pain, in thy pain.
f
f
p
render
p
E- ja Ma- - ter,
Love's sweet foun- -tain,
f
p
p
più p
cresc.
fons a- mo- - ris, fons a- mo- - ris, Me sen- ti- - re
Mo- - ther ten- - der, Mo- - ther ten- - der, Haste, this hard heart
più p
cresc.

f
3
p
vim do- lo- - ris, Fac, ut te- - cum
soft to ren- - der, Make me shar- - er
f
p
mf
p esp.
f
lu- - ge- - am, Fac, ut te- - cum lu- - ge-
in thy pain, Make me shar- - er in thy
p
f
p
pp
-am. E- - ja Ma- - ter, fons a- mo- ris, Me sen-
pain. Love's sweet foun- - tain, Mo- - ther ten- der, Haste, this
pp
cresc.
allarg.
f
-ti- re vim do- lo- ris, vim do- - lo- - ris,
hard heart soft to ren- der, soft to ren- - der,
allarg.
cresc.
f

p
mf
Fac, ut te - - cum lu -
Make me shar - - er in
p
mf
- ge - - am, Fac, ut te - - - cum lu - - ge -
thy pain, Make me shar - - - er in thy
p
f
p
rall.
a tempo
f
p
- am, lu - - ge - am.
pain, in thy pain.
rall.
f
f
p
esp.
f
p
f
p
rall.
f
mf

FAC UT ARDEAT

No. 9 Chorus

Fire me now

*Original key G minor

mp
cresc.
com - pla - - - - - - - - - - - - -
I may
mp
De - - um Ut si - - bi com - - pla - -
flow - - ing, That fa - - vour I may
mp
cresc.
f
(tr)
f
(tr)
f
p(tr)
(tr)
(tr)
(tr)
cresc.
p
p
cresc.

sf
- - - - - - - - ce - - am.
ob - - tain.
f
- - - - ce- am. Fac ut
ob- tain. Fire me
sf
f
f
Fac ut ar - - de - at cor me - - - -
Fire me now with zeal so glow - - - -
ar - - de- at cor me - - - - - - um
now with zeal so glow - - - - - - ing,
mf
mp(tr)
(tr)
cresc.
(tr)
- - - um In a - - - man - - - - - - -
- - - ing, With love so rich
mf
mp
In a - - man - - - - - -
Love so rich
mf
mp
cresc.

cresc.
do Chri- stum, In a man- do Chri- stum
to Je- sus, To Je- sus with love so rich- ly
do Chri- stum De- um, Ut si bi
to Je- sus flow-ing, That fa vour
dim.
De- um, Ut si- bi com- pla- ce- am. Fac ut
flow- ing, That fa- vour I may ob- tain. Fire me
com pla ce- am. Fac
I may ob- tain. Fire
dim.

(tr)
ar- de- at cor me- - - - - - um,
now with zeal so glow- - - - - - ing,
ut ar- - de- at cor me- um, In a-
me now with zeal so glow- ing, Love so
f
mf
dim.
Ut si- bi com-pla- - - - - - - - - ce- -
That fa- vour I may ob- -
mf
-man- do Chri- - stum De- - - - - -
rich to Je- - sus flow- - - - - -
mf
dim.
mp
cresc.
-am. Ut si- - bi com- - - - - -
-tain. That fa- - vour I
mp
-um. Ut si- bi com- pla- - - - - - - - ce-
-ing. That fa-vour I may ob-
mp
cresc.

f
pla - - - - - - - - - - - - ce -
may ob -
f
- am, com - - - - - pla - - ce - am.
- tain, I may ob - tain.
f
mf
- am. Fac ut ar - - de - - - -
- tain. Fire me now with
mf
Fac ut ar - - de - at cor me - um
Fire me now with zeal so glow - ing,
mf
f
- - - - - at cor me - - um, Ut
zeal so glow - - ing, That
mf
f
mf
Ut si - - bi com-pla - - ce - - am, com- pla - - -
That fa - - vour I may ob - - tain, I may
mf
mp

cresc.
f
(tr)
si- bi compla- - - - - - - - - - - -
fa- vour I may
cresc.
mf
p
- - - - - - - - - - - - - - - - - -
cresc.
- - - - - - ce- am. Fac ut ar- de- at cor
ob- tain. Fire me now with zeal so
- - - - - - ce- - am. In a - man- - -
ob- - tain. Fire me, fire
cresc.

ff
me- - - - - - - um,
glow- - - - - - - ing,
Ut
That
ff
- - - - - - - - do
me,
Chri- - - - - stum
That
I
ff
allarg.
si- - - - - bi com- pla- - - - - - -
I fa- - - - vour may
De- - - - - - - um,
fa- - - - - - - vour,
Ut si- bi com-
That fa- vour I
allarg.
a tempo
- - ce- am.
ob- tain.
- pla- ce- am.
may ob- tain.
a tempo
f
rall.
ff

SANCTA MATER

No. 10 Duet

Holy Mother

*Original key E♭ major

*Sing as in Pianoforte accompaniment

mf
Tu - - i
Hate, mis -
(tr)
(tr)
f
p
Na- ti vul- - ne- ra- - ti, vul-ne- - ra- ti, Tam di- -
-pri- sion, scorn, de- ri- - sion, scorn, de- - ri- sion, Thirst as- -
mf
mf
p
mf
mp
-gna-ti pro me pa- ti, Poe- - nas me- cum,
-sail-ing, fail- - ing vi- sion, Rail- - ing, ail- ing,
mf
mp
p
f
f
(tr)
poe- - nas, poe- nas me- - cum di- - -vi-de,
rail- - ing, rail- ing, ail- - ing, deal to me,
f
p
f
(tr)
p

f
f
(tr)
poe - - nas, poe - - nas me - - cum di - - - vi-de.
rail - - ing, rail - - ing, ail - - ing, deal to me.
f
p
f
(tr)
mf
p
Fac me ve - - re
In thy keep - - ing
p
Fac me ve - - re
In thy keep - - ing
(tr)
sfp
mf
te - - cum fle-re, te-cum fle- re, Cru- ci- fi - - xo con - - do-
watch - - ing, weeping, watching, weep- ing, By the Cross may I un-
mf
te - - cum fle-re, te-cum fle- re, Cru- ci- fi - - xo con - - do-
watch - - ing, weeping, watching, weep- ing, By the Cross may I un-
mf
sfp
sf
sfp
sfp

-le - - re, con - - do - - - le - - re, Do - nec e - - go
sleep - - ing, I ___ un - - sleep - ing, Live and sor - - row
-le - - re, con - - do - - - le - - re, Do - nec e - - - - go
sleep - - ing, I ___ un - - - sleep - ing, Live and sor - - - - row
vi - - xe - ro, Do - - nec e - - go,
for His sake, Live and sor - - row,
vi - - xe - ro, Do - - nec e - - go, do -
for His sake, Live and sor - - row, sor -
do - nec e - - go ___ vi - - - xe - ro.
live and sor - - row ___ for His sake.
-nec, do - nec e - - go ___ vi - - - xe - ro.
-row, live and sor - - row ___ for ___ His sake.

mf
Ju - - - xta cru- - cem te- - - cum
Close to Je- - sus, with thee
p
sta- - re,
kneel- ing,
mf
Te li- - - ben- - ter
All thy do- - lours
f
p
p
In plan- - - - - - ctu de-
Oh, grant this, the
p
so- - - ci- - a- - re, In plan- - - - - - ctu de-
with thee feel- - ing, Oh, grant this, the
p

mf
-si- - de- ro, in plan- - ctu, in
prayer I make, Oh grant this, Oh,
-si- - de- ro, in
prayer I make, Oh,
mf p
plan- - - -ctu de- -si- - - de-ro.
grant this, the prayer I make.
plan- - - -ctu de- -si- - - de-ro.
grant this, the prayer I make.
sf
f
Vir- - go vir- gi-num
Maid im- - ma- cu-late,
p

prae- - - cla- ra,
ex- - - cell- ing,
mf
Mi- - hi jam non sis a- -
Peer- - less one, in heaven high
f
p
p
Fac me te- - - cum plan- - - ge-
Make me tru- - - ly mourn with
-ma- -ra; Fac me te- - - cum plan- - - ge-
dwell- ing, Make me tru- - - ly mourn with
sf
p
mf
-re, Mi- hi jam non sis a- ma- -ra; Fac,
thee, Peer- less one, in heaven high dwell- ing, Make,
mf
f
-re, Mi- hi jam non sis a- ma- -ra; Fac,
thee, Peer- less one, in heaven high dwell- ing, Make,
mf
f
sfp
sfp

fac me te- - cum, fac me te - - cum
make me tru- - ly, make me tru- - ly
fac me te - - cum
make me tru- - ly
plan- - ge-re, fac me te- - - cum
mourn with thee, make me tru- - - ly
plan- - ge-re, fac me te- cum, fac me te- - - cum
mourn with thee, make me tru- ly, make me tru- - - ly
rall.
plan- - ge-re.
mourn with thee.
plan- - ge-re.
mourn with thee.
rall.
a tempo
rall.

FAC UT PORTEM

No. 11 Contralto solo *Make me, sighing*

mf
p
cresc.
3
3
pla- - - - - - - - - - - - - - gas
an- - - - - - - - - - - - - - guish
p
cresc.
f
re- - co- le-re.
He bore for me:
f
f
sf
sf
mp
Fac me pla- gis
With the same scars,
sf
p
mf
p
render
mf
p
vul- - ne- -ra- ri, vul- - ne- -ra- ri Cruce
la- - cer- a- ted, la- - cer- -a- ted By the
mf

poco più animato
cresc.
hac i- ne - - bri- a- ri, i- ne - - - bri- a- - ri
cross en- fired, e- la- ted, en- fired, e- la- - ted,
cresc.
a tempo
mf
f
Ob a- - mo- - - - - - - - - rem Fi- li- i, ob a-
Wrought by love to ecs-ta- sy, wrought by
mf
f
sf
3 f (tr)
p sub.
allarg.
3 (tr)
- mo- - rem Fi- - li- i, ob a- mo- - - - rem Fi- - - - li-
love to ecs- - ta-sy, wrought by love to ecs- - - - ta-
f
p sub.
a tempo
f
- i.
-sy.
f
f
allarg.
f
f

INFLAMMATUS

No. 12 Duet

Thus inspired

*Original key B♭ major

SOPRANO
mf
In-flam- - ma- tus et ac- cen- sus
Thus in- - spir- ed and af- fec- ted
p
Per te, Vir-go, sim de- fen- sus In di- - - e ju-
Let me, Vir-gin, be pro- tect- ed, When sounds forth the
(tr)
-di- ci- i. In-flam-ma- - - tus et ac- cen- - sus, Per te,
judg- ment cry. Thus in- spir- - - ed and af- fect- - ed Let me,
cresc
cresc.
Vir- - - go, sim de- fen- - - sus In di- - - - - -
Vir- - - gin, be pro- tect- - - ed When sounds
f
p

f
- - - - - - e ju- - di- - ci- - i.
forth the judg- ment cry.
(tr)
f
mf
cresc.
CONTRALTO
mf
Fac me cru-ce
May the sa- cred
f
p
f
Mor-te Chris-ti pre- mu- ni- - ri
He who died there so be- friend me,
cu- sto- di- ri,
cross de- fend me,
(tr)
(tr)

p (tr)
mf (tr)
Confo- ve- - ri, con-fo- ve- - ri,
That His par- don, that His par- don,
p (tr)
mf (tr)
mf sfp
Con-fo- ve- - ri, con-fo-ve- - ri, con- fo- ve- - - -
That His par- don, that His par- don, that His par- - - -
p (tr)
mf (tr)
mf p
(tr)
cresc. (tr)
(tr)
Fac me cru- ce cu-sto-di- ri, Mor-te Chris- ti
May the sa- cred cross de-fend me, He who died there
(tr)
(tr)
(tr)
cresc.
f (tr)
p
mf
premu-ni- ri, Con- - fo- - ve- - ri, con- fo- ve- - ri
so be-friend me, That His par- - don, that His par- - don
- - - ri, Con- - fo- - ve- - ri, con- fo- ve- - ri
- - - -don, That His par- - don, that His par- - don
(tr)
f
p
mf

f
p
gra - - ti- a, con - - fo - - ve - - ri
shall suf-fice, that His par - - don,
p
gra - - ti- a con - - fo - - ve - - ri
shall suf-fice, that His par - - don,
(tr)
f
mf
p
poco rall.
mf
f
con- fo- ve- - ri gra- - ti- a.
that His par- - don shall suf-fice.
mf
f
con- fo- ve- - ri gra- - ti- a.
that His par- - don shall suf-fice.
poco rall.
mf
f
mf
cresc.
f
mf
cresc.
ff

QUANDO CORPUS

No. 13 Chorus

When this earthly frame

*Original key F minor

mf
mp
mo - ri - e - tur, Fac ut
frame is ri - ven Grant that
mf
cor - pus mo - ri - e - tur,
earth - ly frame is ri - ven,
mf
mp
mf
a - ni - mae do - ne - tur
to my soul be giv - en
mp
Fac ut
Grant that
mf
mp
mf
cresc.
Pa - ra - di -
All the joys
cresc.
a - ni - mae do - ne - tur Pa - ra -
to my soul be giv - en All the
mf
cresc.

f
- - si glo - - - ri - a.
of Pa - - - ra - dise.
f
-di - - si glo - - - ri - a.
joys of Pa - - - ra - dise.
f
p
mp
p sf dim. - - -
Quan - - do cor - - pus mo - - - -
When this earth - ly frame
mp
p sf dim. - - -
Quan - - do cor - - - pus mo - - - -
When this earth - - - ly frame
mp
dim. - - -
pp
cresc.
-ri - - - - e - - - - tur, Fac ut
is ri - - - - ven, Grant that
pp
cresc.
-ri - - - - e - - - - tur, Fac ut
is ri - - - - ven, Grant that
pp
cresc. - - -

f
a - ni - mae do - ne - tur Pa - ra - di - si glo - ri -
to my soul be giv - en All the joys of Pa - ra -
a - ni - mae do - ne - tur
to my soul be giv - en
f
cresc.
allarg.
ff
f
poco più lento
p
- a, Pa - ra - di - si glo - ri - a, Pa - ra -
- dise, All the joys of Pa - ra - dise, All the
p
ff
f
Pa - ra - di - si glo - ri - a,
All the joys of Pa - ra - dise,
allarg.
p
cresc.
ff
f
p
rall.
p
pp
a tempo
di - si glo - ri - a.
joys of Pa - ra - dise.
p
pp
Pa - ra - di - si glo - ri - a.
All the joys of Pa - ra - dise.
rall.
a tempo
rall.
p
pp

AMEN

No. 14 Chorus

*Original key F minor

men, a- - - men, a- men, a- men, a- - - -
men, a- - - men, a- - - - - - -
marc.
men, a- - - - - - - - - - - - - - - - - - - -
men, a- - - - - - - - - - - - - - - - - - -

Printed by Caligraving Ltd., Thetford, Norfolk